MW00379128

Street Portraits

MACK

Street Portraits

Dawoud Bey

Dawoud Bey: Griot With A Camera
Greg Tate

Norman Mailer once proclaimed that he'd never seen "a Negro male over the age of 18 whose face wasn't a work of art." This was Mailer in his hyperbolic "White Negro" phase of the mid 50s (perhaps a lifetime preoccupation given his later writings on boxing, and white male convicts Jack Abbott and Gary Gilmore), a Mailer enthralled by Allen Ginsberg's groundbreaking (and career-making) Whitman meets bebop inspired poem, "Howl" and its incandescent and incantatory opening lines:

> I saw the best minds of my generation destroyed by madness,
>   starving hysterical naked,
> dragging themselves through the negro streets at dawn
>   looking for an angry fix,
> angelheaded hipsters burning for the ancient heavenly
>   connection to the starry dynamo in the machinery of night.

This literary conflation of beauty, brilliance, and the staggering spirit of the negro streets was one that African American novelists were just beginning to recognize as their challenge and their birthright.

One thinks now of Ann Petry's *The Street,* Paula Marshall's *Brown Girl, Brownstones,* Ralph Ellison's *Invisible Man,* James Baldwin's *Go Tell It On The Mountain,* and Chester Himes's *A Rage In Harlem.*

All of these books took up the Olympian task of delivering the vibrancy of the "negro streets" to the page with grandiloquent verisimilitude, rendering the people who daily parade our urban villages with poignant subjective character and vernacular savoir faire.

In this late 50s moment a young Black poet from Newark by way of Howard University, and the air force has made it to the East Village haven of Ginsberg's Beat Generation of "angelheaded hipsters… contemplating jazz".

His name is LeRoi Jones, and in his evolution from Black Beat bard to Black cultural nationalism's literary Moses Imamu Amiri Baraka, he'll generate texts, memes and movements that inspire a generation to embrace "The Black Aesthetic" and "Black Is Beautiful" like cries of war, and a definition of "The Black Arts" as a movement that is as much magical as tribal in spellbinding potential – a field of creative operation as romantically and rhythmically grounded in the grassroots, everyday culture of working Blackfolk and even their more lumpen proletarian cousins.

From a historical vantage, photographed images of Blackfolk, from the 1830s advent of camera technology to the emergence of cinema as mass entertainment in the early twentieth century, has lent the enterprise both a dream and a nightmare aspect.

In his lecture on photography, orator/activist/author/diplomat Frederick Douglass, a man photographed more than anyone else in the 19th century, believed, writes Library of Congress researcher Melissa Lindberg, that

> *by distributing photographs of himself posed and clothed in the manner of his own choosing, Douglass provided alternatives to racist, stereotypical portrayals of African Americans. He acknowledged the power not only of photographs, but of images in general, including political cartoons and other printed formats: 'It is evident, observed Douglas in his essay "Of Pictures and Progress", that the great cheapness, and universality of pictures must exert a powerful though silent influence, upon the ideas and sentiment of present and future generations.'*

Despite Douglass's optimism about the power of photography to democratize and humanize the optics of race in America, less generous takes proliferated in his lifetime.

The earliest photographs taken of enslaved Blackfolk in America were commissioned by Swiss immigrant and Harvard zoologist, Louis Agassiz, a titan among scientific educators in the 19th century, but also a proponent of a white supremacist and pseudoscientific theory of evolution known as "polygenesis" – one that came to be swiftly refuted by Charles Darwin. Aguirre intended for photographic portraiture to demonstrate that people of African descent had evolved from a different branch of the human family than Europeans. In 1850 Agassiz visited several plantations in Columbia, South Carolina to select examples of "pure African stock". He then commissioned noted area portraiture photographer JT Zealy to render studio portraits of the chosen enslaved.

Renty Taylor, born in 1775 in the Congo, and his daughter Delia were made to strip naked in JT Zealy's daguerreotype studio to provide physiognomic proof that Blackfolk were less than human. The photographs so epically failed to deliver the proof of concept Agassiz intended. It's been surmised a devastatingly opposite effect occurred because Zealy shot them with his customary artistry. A chagrined Agassiz only showed them once and abandoned polygenesis as a photographically verifiable classroom lecture topic.

Agassiz donated the photographs to Harvard Peabody Museum in 1873, where they sat in the attic until 1976. They have since been used by the university to promote books and journals. One sees in Zealy's daguerreotypes the capacity of captive Black individuals to confront and take head-on self-possession of their imaging under brutalized and barbaric circumstances. This is why these "hostage photographs" (as Ta-Nehisi Coates indicts them) are able to sear us 170 years later. Artist Carrie Mae Weems brought the Zealy photographs of "Papa" Renty, Delia, and other hostage-subjects to art world attention in her 1995-1996 series "From Here I See What Happened And I Cried", which appropriated and reframed the work and provided anti-racist captions.

The mass media imaging of Blackfolk which proliferated in America from 1865 on was entangled with the denigrating abominations of minstrelsy sheet music, "coon art" in various media, and lynching photographs. The advent of Hollywood brought racist cartoons by Disney, among others, and a century's worth of vile, denigrating, and stereotypical portrayals of Black people in American cinema

The history of Black American photographic studios brought forth by scholars Deborah Willis and Michele Gates Moresi edifies us about a countervailing legacy of corrective, heroic representation as early as 1845. By the 1920s Harlem Renaissance, this tradition had brought forth the luminous studio-portraiture practice of James Van Der Zee. The photographer's longevity until the 1980s would see him make striking and indelibly aristocratic portraits of Jean-Michel Basquiat in Van Der Zee's eerie and ennobling signature style.

By the 1940s the *Life* magazine photojournalism of Gordon Parks would alter forever the quality of imaging of Black Americans in mainstream media.

In the early 1950s the chiaroscuro masterpieces of grandmaster Roy DeCarava arrived to establish an aesthetically refined high bar for photographs of Black subjects that possessed a culturally informed depth. Work reflective, in his words, of "a creative expression, the kind of penetrating insight and understanding of Negroes which I believe only a Negro photographer can interpret."

Dawoud Bey represents the first generation of young Black photographers radicalized by the Black Arts Movement to also fall under the hypnotic sway of DeCarava's work and then forge their own paths to lensing the everyday beauty of the Black community. By the post-revolutionary 1970s there was no miracle or challenge for this generation of artists in seeing the iconographic faces of the Black community as works of art. Instead they faced the test of making art equal to the proliferation of the diverse beauty in the community's DNA.

After a screening of Julie Dash's totemic 1991 feature film *Daughters of the Dust,* cinematographer Arthur Jafa, who'd just won that year's Sundance Festival award, was asked by a startled and bewildered Black audience member, "How did you make everyone look so beautiful?" Jafa modestly replied, "I just shot what was already there."

Beyond technique though, what the audience member was responding to was Jafa's enthralling treatment of dark-skinned Black femininity – a recognition which Black women actors speak of to this day and which is still hardly commonplace on major Hollywood film sets where many do their own make-up, or hire knowledgeable peers, because their skin tones are seen as too problematic for standard industry practitioners. In this pursuit of rendering "what was already there", Jafa was influenced by those of Bey's generation, as well as those of the preceding generation who had formed the Kamoinge collective of Black photographers – a group who by the mid-70s were extracting and emulsifying masterful imagistic narratives from the casually profound 'sweet flypaper' of Black life which DeCarava and Langston Hughes had essayed upon in their book-length collaboration of the same name. The Kamoinge group documented their extensions of DeCarava's genius in a series of monographs published in the 70s as *The Black Photographers Annual*. The years of Bey's street portraits, 1988-1991, coincide with the second presidential term of Ronald Reagan. Within the national Black community that timespan is also commonly referred to as a "the crack era" and "the golden age of hip hop". Neither marker in time is untethered from the occupant of the Oval Office in those years.

The mainstream media's predominant stories about Blackfolk in that time were either about gang murders or drug selling and addiction. Occasionally something might slip in about the activism against apartheid in South Africa or the anti-racist demonstrations being mounted in New York City seeking justice for the killings of unarmed Blackfolk by police and white neighborhood mobs.

There were several plagues and pathological stigmata visited upon the Black community's house in that stretch of years, but did they encompass the whole story for an African American population 40 million strong? Dawoud Bey's *Street Portraits* regally *bid* (and not *beg*) to differ.

The late poet, playwright and scholar Larry Neal once observed that, "To be Black in this country is to always affirm *something*." A truth to which we might add: it is also to always *perform and represent something* in the name of reclaiming the humanity of Blackfolk from the anti-Black hate campaigns of minstrelsy, lynching postcards, coon artefacts, and scholar Donald Bogle's litany of infamous Hollywood stereotypes *Toms, Coons, Mulattoes, Mammies, and Bucks* – not to mention the failed, inhumane intended weaponization of the Zealy daguerreotypes.

In his own documentary film-making practice, Jafa makes a distinction between the collected testimony of those Blackfolk he identifies as "specialists" (creatives and academics, primarily) and those from the communal congregation, whom he cites as "the uncommon folk".

In Bey's practice he is obviously not just the specialist but also the editorial invisible hand.

In poring over his highly selective, captured treasure trove of vibrant and generous Black visages, we observe Bey's repeated pursuit of not just our community's divergent and many-splendored "un-commoners", but also those among them who are already quite well composed – "very pulled together", as the saying goes – and extremely *self-possessed*.

These portraits attest to the power of "the Black gaze" – how Black-folk's eye-to-eye *looking-back* game can meet any righteous or even *reckless eyeballing* judgment the world might bring with an equal and opposing optical Super-Kryptonian heat-visioned (and *haute-visioned*) force – a stare, a glare, an inquiring dare, a wry comeback, an introspective indifference, a casual summation, an audacious insouciance, an Amazonian, eye-rolling snapback.

The emotional range and diversity of personae found in Bey's portraits are rarely represented in cinema, even our own. Nor is the ultra-cool restraint shown by Bey's subjects – the readily apparent refusal to be wildly performative for the camera. This constant of the series speaks to the tremendous sense of trust between Bey and his aesthetically driven choice of uncommon chosen people. His apprehension and comprehension of "The Church of What's Happening Now's" (as per 70s variety host Flip Wilson's famous declamation) framing of the tribe's funk-da-fied, *Drylongso* exceptionalism. Bey's portraits also celebrate Blackfolk's uncommon carriage, forged under multigenerational pressure – the taking of the bold, embodied stance Cornel West once referred to as "Black postural semantics" – how we show up ready for the world adorned and armored with our mean lids, mean shades, and even meaner *leans*.

Anyone who's driven through a Black neighborhood at night with discerning eyes has taken notice of our silhouettes' hyper-visibility in neon-strobed darkness; witnessed how remarkably recognizable we are, even in the eclipse of an urban black-out, from our walks, our strolls, our dips and hips, and stationary swagger; come upon the revelation that one could only be ethnographically clocking the singular movements of subjective *Blacknuss* visible in America.

As you leaf though this monograph we recommend you note the transcendence of social- and class-imposed circumstance and environment pouring through the soulful windows, the corneas and coronas of lensing Minister Bey's curatorially assembled congregation. His photo-sculptural presentation of Black selfhood through fashion, through freeze-frame strut and swagger should inspire your invitation to commune with these magnificently and resplendently uncommon Black spirits centered and circumambulating close to their homes, hoods and indigenous urban habitats beyond the breakadawn.

The photographs in this book were made with the support of a number of parties. Though no longer in existence, the work was initially supported by the Artist Support Program of The Polaroid Corporation under the direction of Barbara Hitchcock. The Visual Studies Workshop, in Rochester, New York provided me with a one month residency during which time I made the photographs in that city included in this book. My thanks to Sean Kelly Gallery, Rena Bransten Gallery, and Stephen Daiter Gallery for their ongoing support of my work, with a special thanks to Stephen Daiter, for his work in bringing this book into being.

Finally, I dedicate this book to my son Ramon, who will now have the opportunity to see just what his dad was doing in the years before he was born.

Dawoud Bey

Street Portraits
Dawoud Bey

First edition published by MACK
©2021 MACK for this edition
©2021 Dawoud Bey for his images
©2021 Gregory Tate for his text

Design by Morgan Crowcroft-Brown
Printed in Italy

978-1-913620-10-3
mackbooks.co.uk

, USA

, USA